CW01652463

Menu:
eds It?

Raymond H. Woolsey

Introduction by
ROBERT H. DUNN, M. D., M. P. H.

REVIEW AND HERALD® PUBLISHING ASSOCIATION
HAGERSTOWN, MD 21740

Abridged, 1988
Revised, 1995
Review and Herald® Publishing Association

Editor: Thomas A. Davis
Cover Design: Harry Knox
Layout: G. W. Busch

Printed in the U.S.A.

R&H Cataloging Service
Woolsey, Raymond H.
Meat on the menu: who needs it?
1. Meat. 2. Vegetariansim. I. Title.
613.26

ISBN 0-8280-0483-8

Contents

Introduction

OUR LIVES are sustained by food, which contains energy produced by the effects of solar radiation on the leaves of plants. A green substance, chlorophyll, found in leaves, utilizes the sun's energy and stores it in the plant. With carbon from the air, combined with water and minerals from the soil, substances are produced that maintain life and activity for both man and animals.

Man can receive his energy supply directly from fruits, vegetables, grains, legumes, nuts, and natural oils, or he can obtain it secondhand, from meat or animal products. Because of our relatively inefficient energy transfer mechanisms, a vegetarian utilizes one tenth of the energy stored in his food, while a meat eater utilizes from meat only one hundredth of the energy that was originally stored in the primary source, the plants. This loss is considerable and causes some concern.

It was formerly believed that food and fossil fuels storing energy from the sun were unlimited and could be used without thought or planning. However, with overpopulation, gross mismanagement, and natural catastrophes, our world is facing an imminent energy crisis. Can we continue the great food energy loss by producing meat as a major dietary source for the citizens of the world? Concern over this question has produced a ground swell of interest in plant sources of food as a major approach to solving our ecological crisis.

Raymond H. Woolsey has reviewed the advantages and appropriateness of obtaining food from plant sources. Futher, he has outlined certain disadvantages that may be found in the eating of meat. I have known the author as a personal friend for fifteen years. He has written a number of books and for six years was editor of a health journal. I feel confident the reader will profit from this study of our food sources.

Robert H. Dunn, M.D., M.P.H.
Director of Preventive Medicine
Washington Adventist Hospital

1

Let Reason Rule

A TESTIMONIAL DINNER was being planned to honor England's famous playwright George Bernard Shaw. The host felt it expedient to ask Shaw, a vegetarian, whether he would be offended if meat were served to the other guests. "Oh, no," Shaw replied. Then his eyes twinkled. "I might not be able to hear the good things said about me if everyone were crunching celery sticks!"

Vegetarians are making more noise, and the meatless diet is making more sense, than at any previous time in history. Some of the "noise" is from nutritionists who are making scientific studies on how much protein the body needs and the best places to get it. Some is coming from researchers such as Ralph Nader's "raiders," who report on studies on additives and contamination in flesh food. Much noise is being generated by those who have their eyes on the exploding population and the ability of this planet to produce enough food for everyone.

But perhaps you are simply concerned with the high price of meat the supermarket, and you are looking for economical substitutes to stretch your food budget. Whatever your motive, you have a lot to gain and nothing to lose in examining the meatless diet.

Today there are several kinds of vegetarians. The "pure" vegetarian (sometimes called a vegan) uses no animal product in his dietary—no milk, no eggs, and some do not even use honey. The lactovegetarian does not eat flesh but will add milk and milk products to his fruit, vegetables, grains, and nuts. The lacto-ovo-vegetarian will also include eggs.

Aside from those incensed at the high cost of meat, the group that is presently giving the most publicity to the vegetarian diet are those who look at the question from a moral standpoint. Many people, including those in the youth culture, are concerned about the morality of taking life. We cannot give life, they say, so why should we take it?

Vegetarianism is as old as man. Milton, Pope, Shelley, Voltaire, Thoreau, Franklin, Tolstoy, Wesley, Gandhi, Newton, Rousseau, Kellogg, St. Francis of Assisi—all extolled vegetarianism. So did the early Church Fathers: Chrysostom, Clement of Alexandria, Origen, Tertullian. And on back into the pre-Christian era: Buddha, Asoka, Aristotle, Socrates, Plato, Pythagoras, Ovid, Plutarch—they all advocated a fleshless diet to some degree.

In the Bible the record goes back even further, and it is based not altogether on a moral footing. At Creation, God established that man should live on fruits, grains, and nuts. Later, vegetables were added to the dietary. (See Genesis 1:29; 3:18.) Only when the Flood destroyed vegetation for a period, was man given permission to use flesh (Genesis 9:3). The results of this change of diet were soon evident in man's longevity. Whereas previously man lived for nine hundred years or more, within two or three generations after the Flood he could expect only one hundred to one hundred fifty years, and this soon dwindled to the proverbial "threescore years and ten."

Then there is the question of raising animals for the purpose of slaughtering them. If killing is bad, is not breeding and raising for the purpose of killing even worse?

When the high cost of grain feed forced poultry growers to destroy freshly hatched chicks, the destruction process was portrayed on television as a news item. Thousands of telephone calls protested the slaughter. Yet most of those same callers would gladly eat those same chickens were they allowed to grow a bit. Strange how our morals dim where our dinners are concerned.

And what is happening to our sensibilities while all this slaughter is going on? Can we eat a slaughtered animal without sharing in the slaughter itself? And can we kill creature after creature without our sense of values being affected? Psychiatrists tell us that watching many murders on television has a Pavlovian conditioning effect on us. Are animals so far removed that killing them does not have a similar effect?

Another writer emphasizes still another aspect:

"The use of flesh meat has a tendency to animalize the nature, and to rob men and women of the love and sympathy which they should feel for every one. We are built up from that which we eat, and those whose diet is largely composed of animal food are brought into a condition where they allow the lower passions to assume control of the high powers of the being."[1]

So much for the ethics of the matter. Perhaps these arguments have not turned you on, for not everyone views life through the same color of glasses. There are yet other reasons that merit your attention. When you add them all together they can hardly be ignored, especially as your health and even perhaps your life itself are at stake.

2

"What's to Eat?"

WHEN YOU woke up this morning this planet had about 86,000 more mouths to feed than when you went to bed last night. There are 258,000 more people than there were this time yesterday. They, too, will be looking for something to eat. Meanwhile, the food supply has not gone up comparably. Some improvements have been made in crop development—plant varieties and harvesting technology—but at the same time crop lands have been swallowed up in housing subdivisions. The deserts are still arid, the rain forests are still impenetrable, and the Antarctic is still frozen. There has been talk of "farming" the oceans of plankton and algae, but that still is only talk. And DDT in the ocean waters is disturbing the growth of plankton.[1] There is even talk of growing synthetic proteins on petroleum—but the world's petroleum supply is limited.

Important new varieties of crops have helped to improve the ability of arable lands to produce food, but population is outstripping technology.

Americans have enjoyed a sufficient supply of grain crops and have been able to export to other countries—until recently. Gone are the days of huge surpluses. Even a moderate setback in the weather can—and has—cut back the shipment of wheat to India or of soybeans to Japan, with disastrous effects on the economies of those countries and to the balance of trade with our country. Already half the world suffers from malnutrition.

The President's Science of Advisory Committee says curtly, "The world food problem is not a future threat. It is here and now." [2] In short, we have a food crisis on our hands. That is one reason maritime nations have unilaterally increased their territorial sea limits—to guard their food resources. Iceland is claiming a fifty-mile limit to protect her fishing industry, and British fishermen have protested that claim, to the point of a shooting war. Similar tensions are building among fleets off Newfoundland and in the Pacific.

With this world food shortage in mind, let us consider our options. We could all eat a little less. But with half the world already undernourished, that is not realistic. Or we could change our food pattern. And here there is room for improvement. There is only about two-thirds of an acre of agricultural land on this earth, per person, at the present population level. One fourth of an acre or less is needed to feed a person if he lives on a vegetarian diet. But three acres or more are needed if he depends on animal protein for food.[3] While one acre will produce, as beef, 77 days' worth of protein for a man, the same acre would produce 236 days of protein in milk, 877 days in whole wheat, or 2,224 days in soybeans.[4]

A beef animal must consume one hundred calories to produce ten calories in meat. It takes twenty-one pounds of protein fed to cattle to get one pound of protein in return. Pigs and chickens do a little better, but averaging all classes of food animals, eight pounds of protein in feed are required to get one pound of protein in return.[5]

Another way of looking at it: Eighteen million tons of protein are lost in this feed-to-meat transaction each year in the United States alone. If this wasted protein could have been fed directly in the form of cereal to the world's starving, it would have met 90 percent of the world's protein deficiency.[6]

Cattle and other ruminants could be fed substances that are humanly inedible—they have enzymes in their multiple stomachs that can make use of such substances. But in order to speed them off to market, they are fed high-protein, humanly edible corn, sorghum, oats, barley, soybeans, wheat, and rye.

(Also included in the diet of animals raised for food are the by-products of the slaughterhouse: bone meal, feather meal, blood meal, tankage. The meat industry wants clearance to use "sterilized" chicken manure as animal feed, which would reduce feed costs 60 per cent. Talk about "organic" food![7])

One half of United States harvested land is planted with crops to feed animals; in addition, nearly a million tons of fish products are used to feed animals each year.[8] An administrator in the United States Department of Agriculture declared that the billion or so people in the developed countries use practically as much cereals as feed to produce animal protein as the 4 billion people in other countries use directly as food.[9]

Another matter: More and more, water is being recognized as a resource in short supply and must be conserved. An all-vegetarian regiment requires 300 gallons of water daily for each person. A mixed animal and vegetable diet requires 2,500 gallons daily per person. The cost of water per pound of meat is 25 times that of the cost per pound of vegetarian food.[10]

The President's Science Advisory Committee observes, "Balancing the advantages against the disadvantages of producing animal foods for human beings indicates that the production of animal foods cannot be justified on an economic basis except in special cases."[11]

But would we suffer nutritionally if we used vegetable protein? We will study this aspect more particularly later—and it deserves careful attention. But while we are on a global topic we might note that in Russia only 28 per cent of their crops are fed to animals, whereas in the United States 78 per cent of our grain goes to animals. Yet the protein in the average Russian's diet is about the same as in ours.[12]

Whole races of peoples eat largely of a vegetarian diet, and many are healthier than Americans. Some of these are vegetarians by choice and some by economic necessity. The Jains are an elite group in India—definitely not among the starving masses—yet they do not eat meat. The Hunzas of northern Pakistan, who eat little meat, enjoy remarkable longevity and freedom from disease.

Someone might ask, "Wasn't man biologically designed to eat meat?" Some writers have drawn that conclusion from a superficial examination (often based on medical diagrams only) of the digestive apparatus of man as compared with carnivorous and herbivorous animals. In many ruminants the bowel is long and convoluted, apparently to give the digestive enzymes room and time to break down the plant fibers in the animal's diet. By contrast, most carnivores have large, short, and comparatively smooth bowels. This, it has been reasoned, is because their systems must get rid of flesh as soon as possible, because of its inherent danger of putrefaction and also because of the toxic wastes in flesh.

It so happens that the human colon, when viewed in an anatomical chart, seems short, like that of the carnivore. "Aha," says the flesh advocate, "that demonstrates that man was designed to be a meat eater."

But not so fast. Closer examination of the human colon will show that in actuality it is a rather long organ, after all, that has been foreshortened by three ribbonlike muscles that run its length. In other words, it is "stretchable." This makes an ideal organ for digesting a diet varied by fruits, grains, nuts, and vegetables. On the other hand, because of the time necessary for the normal movement of food along its length, putrefaction and toxic wastes in flesh present a potential danger to the human being.

More evidence of a circumstantial nature comes from the dental structure of man. Whereas carnivorous animals have fangs for tearing and slicing meat, man has incisors for biting fruit and vegetables, and molars for chewing grains, nuts, and vegetables. The following observation was made in a paper presented at an American Heart Association council on atherosclerosis:

"Examination of the dental structure of modern man reveals

that he possesses all of the features of a strictly herbivorous animal. While designed to subsist on vegetarian foods, he has perverted his dietary to accept the food of the carnivore. It is postulated that man cannot handle carnivorous food like the carnivore. Herein may lie the basis for the high incidence of human atherosclerotic disease."[13]

Another aspect of the physiology picture is whether the digestive process itself is not more difficult for the human being than for the animal carnivore. In a study with a dog equipped with a Pavlov pouch (a device for studying the stomach processes of a live animal) researchers found that the quantity, duration, and acidity of gastric juice was greater in the digestion of meat than of vegetarian foods.[14] This would indicate a greater stress on the lining of the stomach and intestines.

But it is time we examine meat itself, which we will do in the next few chapters. Then we will see whether we have viable alternatives.

3

What is Meat?

Americans are getting to be more and more conscious of what they eat. And it is a good thing. They have the best food supply of any people in the world, but they are not necessarily the best fed, because many do not choose to eat the best that is available. Instead they fill up on a lot of "empty" calories, sweets, and starches, and processed foods that have had many of the nutrients refined out of them.

Of course, there are a few hardy souls who go in for the gourmet items—canned rattlesnake meat, fried grasshoppers, chocolate-coated ants. Americans are not the only ones with exotic tastes, either. The French love snails (which could be compared to oysters, aesthetically); Filipinos cherish coddled eggs (with an embryo chicken or duck inside); and the Chinese in Singapore consider newborn mice, dipped in honey, quite a delicacy.

As somebody once said, "There's no accounting for people's tastes." But let's make an accounting for some of the common foods that find their way to our table. There's that beefsteak, for instance. What is it? It is a slice of tissue from a cow. The cow ate wheat and corn and oats and soybeans. These foods passed through the cow's stomachs and intestines. Proteins were broken down, rebuilt, and deposited as tissue about the body, and that's what is on our plate. But that is not all.

The elements in the food were carried by the bloodstream to the liver for processing. Those elements that could not be used, plus the breakdown products of the old dead cells, were carried to the kidneys for elimination. At the time the cow was butchered these processes stopped in their tracks. The section of beef, then, in addition to the protein and fat in the tissue, also contains the toxic waste materials the animal had not eliminated, such as urea (predominating) and uric acid. (And if these sound like urine, you're on the right track. After passing through the kidney's that's what they are.) Other substances include creatinine, creatine, and phenolic acids. [1]

We human beings have these in our own systems as well, to be eliminated by our organs. The addition of the animal's toxic wastes to our own adds to the load our kidneys have to bear.

Studies have been made to determine the effect of high concentrations of urea in the blood. Human patients reported headaches, dizziness, apathy, fatigue. More studies with dogs revealed a progression from weakness to diarrhea, to bowel hemorrhage, as the urea level rose. [2]

Don't kid yourself that these wastes are all drained off when the carcass is bled. The bleeding is not all that complete, even in "kosher" meats. Meat owes most of its flavor to these wastes. If the animal were really well bled and the tissues washed, the meat would be almost tasteless.

And there is another ingredient not often thought of. Most animals are killed in a state of fear. Even when "humanely" slaughtered, after first being stunned by electric shock, captive-bolt pistol, or what have you, they have picked up a general sense of fear from their environment and fellow animals, and have been pouring adrenalin and other hormones into their systems. Adrenalin is a powerful stimulating agent that raises the blood pressure—it is used by the body to prepare for an emergency. It has been said that if a person could remain really angry long enough, his own adrenalin would kill him. Perhaps here is one reason why a meat diet has the effect of animalizing the nature of the eater—why watchdogs fed raw meat are prone to be more vicious than those fed dog biscuits. And it may have something to do with temper, lust, and other personality problems in human beings. It may indeed be true that "you are what you eat."

Along with the waste products in the animal's tissues that were halted in the process of elimination, there may also be dead and virulent bacteria that were harbored in the animal's intestinal tract and that passed into the tissue. Then there may well be fecal matter that contaminated the tissue during the slaughtering process.[3] All this may be included in the steak that is lying there, hot and sizzling, on the plate.

From the same animal may come a few gourmet items that are not so exotic. There's the liver. Doctors tell mothers it's good for them, and mothers tell children it's good for them, and all dutifully eat it. But is it so good? The liver is high in iron content, yes. But it is also the organ assigned the task of changing food elements into forms usable by the body. (Remember the cow's organs were not designed for man's food, but were designed for the cow's benefit.) Many elements the body cannot use are trapped in the liver and remain there. Higher concentrations of mercury and artificial hormones, to name a few, are found in the liver than in other parts of the body. This is where the urea is formed, and the kidneys are where it is separated from the reusable elements. Eating liver and kidneys is eating the animal's disposal system!

And what about that breakfast sausage, or the frankfurter for lunch? Those are processed meats; they have been through a factory, so we will have to go to a factory to see what they really are. A meat-processing plant is a business, so it is expected to make a profit. That means cutting down on expenses, eliminating waste. Spelled out, it means when an animal is butchered you use the whole thing. The hide is sold to a tannery. Hoofs and bones go for fertilizer or animal feed. The intestinal lining is used for frankfurters and sausage skins. And into these frankfurters and sausages go many of the odds and ends of the animal—eyes, ears, bladders, lips, udders, snouts, and parts of bone and skin.[4]

We wouldn't think of eating these organs served to us on a plate, but when they have passed through a grinder not even a meat inspector can tell from what part of the body they came—it is all meat tissue, and all legal.

Westerners profess to be too "civilized" to eat horse, dog, cat, and rat meat. (Many Asians eat these, and after all, there is no apparent difference in the meat itself.) Yet from other animals they will eat the heart, brains, lungs, tongue, tail, lengths of intestines, blood, et cetera. Most people are so accustomed to eating these that they don't give it a second thought—in fact they have to think twice to eat vegetables. So far have we come from man's original diet!

4

Hitchhikers in the Kitchen

THREE HUNDRED people celebrating a bar mitzvah come down sick with intense abdominal pain. Most of them are hospitalized. Food poisoning. An investigation by health authorities determines the culprit to be the smoked whitefish served at the dinner. The real culprit was *Salmonella java,* a bacterium that can infest food at any place along the processing line—container, knives, cooking pot, human hands.

In the bar mitzvah case, the bacteria were traced back through the processing plant in New Jersey to the packing plant on the shores of Great Slave Lake in Canada. The rivers that flow into that lake in the far north were contaminated by people living along their banks. This water was used to wash the fish after they had been disemboweled, and then the fish was packed in ice made from the same river water.

For as long as man has been using meat as food, he has had a problem of preserving it. He has tried smoking it and drying it, and, in more modern times, canning it and freezing it. But these methods—even the modern ones—are not foolproof against some of the organisms that invade meat.

The trouble is that flesh is just about the best medium there is for the growth and culture of bacteria. In fact, in laboratories when researchers want to grow bacteria for study, they usually use some form of meat produce as a culture medium. Adding to the problem is the thickness and the density of some types of meat—ham, for instance. The outside may be well done while the inside has gotten little more than warm. Drying and smoking get rid of much of the moisture and make the meat less susceptible to spoilage. But these processes do not kill all the microbial organisms.

Salmonellosis is one of the more common forms of food poisoning from bacteria organisms. Its symptoms may include abdominal pain, diarrhea, nausea, vomiting, for a period of one to eight days. In cases of infants or the elderly it may be fatal. Twenty-five people died in the space of forty-eight hours in a Baltimore nursing home. An estimated 4 million Americans annually suffer from the disease, at a cost of $600 million. These figures are estimates, because many cases go unreported—most of the reports come from only three states.

The vast majority of salmonella cases in human beings are food-borne, from animals and animal products. Salmonella organisms most frequently occur on and in poultry, eggs, beef, pork, and fish. (Cooking an egg will usually kill the bacteria. But if you open and eat a raw egg, as in an eggnog, there is the chance of bacteria from the outside of the shell contaminating the egg white.)

Contamination runs in cycles: a contaminated animal is taken to the slaughterhouse where it infects the knives, tables, carts, aprons, et cetera, used there. The contamination continues into the by-products, such as bone meal, blood meal, feather meal, meat scraps, tankage, which are fed to other animals.

And just how prevalent is the contamination? In a Massachusetts survey 50.2 per cent of the market poultry were found to have salmonella, and 30 per cent of the tins of frozen eggs.[2] In this same study, 50.8 per cent of the birds from Government-inspected plants were found contaminated. (The contamination rate was 48.7 per cent for the uninspected plants.)[3] In one plant operating under USDA (United States Department of Agriculture) inspection, as high as 95 per cent of the output was contaminated with salmonellae![4]

A strain of bacteria discovered only in 1983 is emerging as a major cause of food poisoning. *E. coli* 0157.H7 in hamburgers caused several deaths and the hospitalization of hundreds of people in the Northwest in 1993. The next year saw the number of outbreaks nationally nearly double. In addition to beef, the bacteria may be found in lamb, pork, and poultry.[5]

Along with the general trend of the American food purchaser to buy his food already processed and ready to eat, is the growing practice of offering meat already barbecued. Barbecuing itself is not conducive to thoroughly cooked meat, and, in addition, the storage temperature in the supermarket is often not cold enough to retard germ growth. A study of staphylococcus food poisoning included the following observation:

"Barbecued meats are being used at an increasing rate. These foods are ideal substrates for the growth of food-poisoning bacteria, may be contaminated readily after barbecuing, and are frequently stored, after cooking, at temperatures ideal for bacterial growth." [6]

Another form of food poisoning, botulism, is also caused by bacteria, one or more of the *Clostridium* varieties. Like the salmonellae, these bacteria may be very prevalent—up to 88 per cent of the fish in the Green Bay area of Lake Michigan were found to be harboring it.[7] Smoking the fish or meat will not kill all these bacteria. Freeze dehydration and rehydration at room temperature does not destroy them. It has been found, with the latter process, that a significant number of microbes still survive. Following the rehydration the spores are still capable of rapid growth and "could lead to tragic results." [8] Not even cooking is a complete safeguard against *Clostridium.*

In all fairness, it should be repeated that occasionally botulin will form in canned vegetables and other processed foods. But most cases of bacterial "food-poisoning" are traceable to animal products.

In addition to the organisms that cause food poisoning, many other diseases may be transmitted from animal to man. Those most commonly transmitted by eating animal products include tuberculosis, tularemia (rabbit fever), hepatitis, and brucellosis (contagious abortion), which becomes undulant fever in man.

Man is not highly susceptible to foot-and-mouth disease, but he can get it from animals and animal products.[9] The virus is usually rendered inactive by the chemical changes inherent in the ripening process of meat. (Ripening refers to the practice of hanging meat up for a few days. The stiffness of rigor mortis gives way and the meat becomes soft and relaxed. It is actually the beginning of putrefaction.) Quick freezing, by eliminating the ripening, suspends the chemical changes that would kill the virus, so they may survive for several months in certain parts of the carcass (liver, kidney, lymph nodes).[10] But even the chemical changes of ripening may not reach into the lymph nodes, large blood clots, and bone marrow of the carcass. Nor do the commercial procedures of boning, salting, and storing render the meat free of these viruses.[11]

Poultry may be more dangerous to man than are animals. Twenty-six diseases are known to be common to both man and fowl, including salmonellosis, staphylococcus, and psittacosis.[12]

From viruses and bacteria we turn to parasites, for which flesh is a natural carrier and host. Most notorious of these parasites are the trichina worms. Spiral-shaped, they live out their life cycle in the pig, getting into the pig's body through his food, multiplying in his blood stream, encysting themselves in this tissue, casting out young in the feces, at which time they are ready to begin the cycle again. In heavily infested herds they may be found around the pen, on the feed crops, and all over the farm.

Uncooked and inadequately cooked pork, especially in the form of "country sausage" and hamburger, is the usual source of infection of human beings. Meat pies, hors d'oeuvres, and other uncooked meat products are also likely carriers.

When the human host eats infected meat, if the meat is well cooked he may be eating several thousand of these dead parasites with each mouthful. If the meat is raw or undercooked (which often is the case) the parasites are released from their pork host and are free to take up new residence in the human being. They make their way to muscle tissue, to the heart, and to the brain. Attacked by the body's defense system, they embarricade themselves in hard cysts, which may weaken the tissue. If there are enough of them they can damage the heart or the brain, or debilitate the muscle. Sometimes the cysts burst, releasing thousands of small fry into the system. Then the host comes down with trichinosis. The doctor may diagnose it correctly, or he may not.

Symptoms will vary with the progress of the parasites through the body system. As the larvae penetrate the duodenal and jejunal epithelium (in the first part of the small intestine) the body reacts in nausea, vomiting, diarrhea, colic. When the larvae are in the process of migrating to muscle tissue, they produce muscular pains, difficulty in breathing, chewing, and speech. Enlarged lymph glands, encephalitis, meningitis, and edema around the eyes may occur. As the parasites encyst, they may cause toxic edema (water-filled swellings) and extreme dehydration. The blood pressure falls rapidly and the patient collapses. There may be damage to the brain, peripheral neuritis, and defects of vision. Complications from the disease may include lobar pneumonia, peritonitis, pleurisy, and nephritis.[13]

A disease similar to trichinosis, yet which is only recently coming to public notice, is toxoplasmosis. It usually causes no serious harm in adults but is a serious problem among newborns. As many as one in 1,000 births may be infected with this disease.[14] As a cause of congenital defects it outranks rubella, muscular dystrophy, congenital syphilis, and phenylketonuria (PKU), a disease for which all new babies are routinely tested.[15] No one knows how many abortions or stillbirths are caused by it.

The toxoplasmosis parasite is crescent-shaped and very tiny—thousands of them can get on the head of a pin. Like trichinae, the parasite is passed to human beings in raw and undercooked meat—rare hamburgers or steaks, hors d'oeuvres, Italian salami. This parasite also makes its sexual cycle in house cats. Handling their feces (as emptying the litter basket) can infect a human being.

In the human body these parasites invade the cells—every kind of cell except the red blood cell. But they have a special affinity for the nerve cells of the brain, spinal column, and the eyes—the cells that do not regenerate themselves.

In adult human beings, the symptoms of toxoplasmosis are often vague and difficult to diagnose. In some respects they are similar to mononucleosis (a washed-out feeling). The disease sometimes results in enlarged lymph glands, suggesting Hodgkin's disease, and on occasion may destroy the eye. Babies born with the disease may be blind or have some brain abnormality. In a few people, the organisms run wild instead of encysting, resulting in heart attacks, blindness, brain damage, or death. Severity of the disease depends on the virulence of the strain, the dose, and resistance of the human host.

And how prevalent is toxoplasmosis in the world? Clinicians at Cornell University Medical College place the estimate at 500 million to one billion human carriers, and at least that many infected animals and birds. In one Japanese city, one fourth of the population was found infected. A similar proportion was found in Portland, Oregon, while a third of those examined in New Orleans had it.[16] This indicates that many people eat infected meat that is undercooked.

Half of the mothers who are infected during pregnancy pass the parasites on to their babies.[17]

All of these parasites, and practically all of the food-poisoning microbes, are a danger to man only as he eats meat and meat products. How much safer it is to make vegetables our dietary, and leave the bugs to themselves.

But why isn't the government doing something about this? one may ask. Surely meat inspection should prevent such infected meat from reaching the family table. The stamp of "U.S. Inspected" should ensure wholesome fare. But the matter is not that simple, as we shall see in the next chapter.

5

Where Are the Inspectors?

SINCE 1907 the federal government has concerned itself with the quality of meat sold commercially. But for many years its concern was limited only to meat that crossed state lines. Some states had their own inspection system for meat, although their standards often were not equal to federal standards. But sixteen states did not inspect at all, and others merely licensed slaughterhouses.

With the buildup of interest in consumer welfare in the 1960s, documented evidence compiled by federal meat inspectors, and assists from consumer organizations, the Wholesome Meat Act of 1967 was passed. This required all states to either accept federal inspection in all their meat-processing plants, or to come up to United States standards within two years.

But laws don't make meat wholesome. The laws have to be enforced, and therein lies part of the problem—the human element. The agency charged with inspection of meat is the Consumer and Marketing Service of the United States Department of Agriculture (USDA). Here we have a classic example of "politicians making strange bedfellows." The same agency that has the responsibility of protecting the public from unwholesome meat also has the responsibility of promoting meat production. Meat producers and processors have stronger financial resources and political lobbies than do consumers, and so when interests conflict the USDA is likely to lean toward the former.[1]

The Government Accounting Office (GAO) checked up on the USDA inspection program in 1971, by examining sixty-eight poultry plants. These plants accounted for 19 per cent of all poultry processing. The GAO found "unacceptable" sanitation conditions in "most of them—dirty equipment, inadequate pest control, dirty floors, walls, and overhead structures. In thirty-five plants the GAO found poultry products contaminated with fecal matter, digestive tract contents, bile, feathers.[2]

In 1993 the USDA temporarily shut down 30 large slaughterhouses because of unacceptable amounts of fecal contamination. Twelve of the 30 were placed under intensified scrutiny. Interestingly, the packing industry says the inspectors themselves may be to blame for some of the contamination.[3]

But what does inspection mean, anyway? Meat inspectors make periodic checks of the fat and water content of the meat (these affect the consumer's pocketbook) and ocular examinations for any obviously diseased parts, such as a tumor or open sore.[4] But while they no doubt do their best, they do not and cannot make laboratory examinations of each bird, fish, or animal. Says a veterinarian:

"It takes a physician and a clinical laboratory 24 hours or more to determine the causative organism of infection in a human being. In poultry and meat inspection as practiced in this country by the Federal Government, a layman is expected, in as little as two seconds, to determine the wholesomeness and freedom from infection of the meat of a chicken, cow, sheep, or pig that we are to eat. It is impossible."[5]

Consider a typical poultry plant. Five lay inspectors (with from one to six weeks' training), operating under an inspector in charge, must examine 48,000 birds daily. The birds pass by on a conveyor belt at the rate of one hundred a minute, giving the inspectors about three and one-half seconds per bird. All he can do is look at it, feel it, and perhaps smell it. And all this in the midst of distractingly noisy and dangerous machinery.

All the birds go into a chiller after being eviscerated (the entrails removed). In the chiller, which can hold 4,800 birds at a time, one bird with a high bacteria count can contaminate the whole lot. Similarly, one trichinae-infected hog crossing a butcher's block can infect many more carcasses.

What happens when an inspector happens to see some diseased part? The diseased part is cut out, and the rest of the body is OK'd with the inspection stamp. Were it not for a slip of the tongue by a USDA official during a press conference, which set up a hue and cry by the public, even cancerous parts might now be included in sausage. After all, was the argument, it has not been proved that animal cancers can cause cancer in man, and cooking *might* kill the germs.[6]

From where do the inspectors get the standards for which they aim? Most of these are set arbitrarily. Recent consumer agitation, backed by the concern of the medical profession, tried to get the fat content of hamburgers reduced to 25 per cent. The meat industry held out for 33 per cent and even 35 per cent. The USDA settled for 30 per cent.[7]

Water content in chickens was set at 12 per cent at a time when packing plants were using ice to chill the chicken carcasses. With new methods they can chill with only 7 or 8 per cent water absorption—but the old standard still stands, and plants actually take steps to keep the water level up to 12 per cent.[8] In another anomaly, "all meat" franks can contain, by law, in addition to 30 per cent fat, 10 per cent *added* water. But they must not contain dried milk or nonfat dry milk, even though this would add additional protein to the nutrition quality.[9]

Sometimes standards are lowered to meet industry demand. In Montana, for instance, the "safe" level of pesticide residue in milk was adjusted upward when the residue levels began to approach those previously set as "safe." The FDA (Food and Drug Administration, another "watchdog agency," under the Department of Health, Education, and Welfare) in 1973 doubled the amount of arsenic over what was previously allowed in poultry. Arsenic is added to chicken and hog food to speed up their growth.[10]

Then there is the case of a major soup packing plant. Running its own tests on turkeys it had bought bearing the USDA inspection approval, the firm found the birds had illegal amounts of heptachlor epoxide, a pesticide. The USDA ran a top-secret test and found 350,000 birds affected, some with 34 times the permissible level of heptachlor.[11] These birds would have been sold for Thanksgiving dinner if the soup company had relied on the official assurance of "wholesomeness." We can thank the soup company for its alertness.

But most laws relating to wholesome meat apply only to their processing. Some local laws also apply to sanitary conditions in the places where the meat is sold to the public. But as for the meat itself, once it is stamped inspected, the consumer is on his own to make sure he is buying edible meat. All he has to go by is sight and sometimes smell, but usually the latter is inoperable because the meat has been prepackaged. So the customer is at the mercy of the meat market operator, who will try to move all the meat he can at the highest price he can get.

For instance, there is the matter of labeling and pricing. "U.S. Prime" does not mean it is the best meat available. It merely designates that the fat content is high.[12] Many stores classify ground beef as chuck, round, and sirloin. But the fat and protein content of the beef may be the same. The classification depends on what the store owner wants to push that day, or what he feels the market will stand. Any difference is in packaging and pricing—the remainder is psychological.[13]

You might expect spoiled meat in a market to be discarded, and that is what the *Journal of the American Medical Association* warns should be done.[14] But that doesn't make for "economical management," according to the market owners. A correspondent who worked for fifteen years in a series of stores in a grocery chain describes how meat is "managed." After a ham remains in the display case too long, flecks of mold appear on the surface. The ham is washed under hot water in a sink. If the workers are busy the ham may be allowed to remain in the sink water for several hours, although the water will cool. Eventually the ham is rewrapped and put back for sale. This is repeated as often as necessary. If still unsold, the ham is ground up with pork, hot spices, and barbecue powder, and sold as "deluxe ham loaf." "The *only* reason barbecue powder is put on this meat is that the color, odor, and taste of it need to be disguised."[15]

If chicken doesn't sell, it is cut up and sold at higher prices as "more tender," "choice bits." Sometimes such offerings will be advertised as "Packed Fresh in This Store Daily," which is correct when you understand the packing is fresh, not the chicken.

The same source reports that barbecued chicken or spare ribs are those that are so spoiled they won't sell from the "fresh meat" counter. "I've never seen a fresh wholesome piece of meat cooked in one of these rotisserie ovens." Of course, in some stores by special order you can select a piece of meat or chicken and have it barbecued while you wait. *(Consumer Reports* recommends that chuck be ground to order, or ground at home.)[16]

The following account is from hearings before a Senate investigating committee. On the West Coast a major, brand-name, nationally famous meat packer disclosed that as common practice it sold meat on a commission basis. If the retailer did not sell the meat it was returned to the packer who repacked and recirculated the meat to the markets. Reasons for returning included "moldy, sour, discolored, off-condition, slick and slimy." The packer accepted spare ribs, for instance, returned for sliminess, discoloration, and stickiness. They were "rejuvenated" by curing and smoking and given the upbeat name of Windsor Loins. These were sold in ghetto stores for more than the price of fresh pork chops. Vandenberg Air Force Base and inner-city stores were the prime market for this meat.[17]

Consumer Reports magazine made a study of the quality of hamburgers available to the average consumer. They purchased 126 samples of ready-ground hamburger, mostly in the Philadelphia area but some on the West Coast and elsewhere. They tested this hamburger meat, and here is what they reported:

"Food technologists generally agree that putrefaction has set in when the (bacteria) count reaches 10 million bacteria per gram of hamburger. By that measure, about 20 per cent of the 126 ready-ground samples we analyzed for total bacteria count had begun to spoil. One obviously putrefied sample tested out at 180 million bacteria per gram."[18]

Because coliform bacteria usually indicate fecal contamination (and thus the likely presence of disease-causing organisms) scientists have set low limits for this form of bacteria in food—some states as low as ten coliforms per gram. The U.S. Public Health Service has about the same limit on pasteurized milk. Using 100 coliform per gram of hamburger as a starting point, the *Consumer Reports* survey reported 21 per cent of their Philadelphia-purchased samples assayed at 100-1,000 per gram, and 52 per cent had higher than 1,000 coliforms per gram.[19]

Well, all these bacteria and viruses and parasites that are in meat "just come naturally." That's the nature of meat; it spoils easily. We can't really blame USDA inspectors for passing defective meat. Theirs is literally an impossible task. But for that same reason we cannot complacently accept that all meat we may buy is wholesome simply because it has been "inspected." As Dr. Sussman said, "It is impossible."

Let us next consider some of the things man or man's environment has added to meat.

6

. . . And Alphabet Soup

A SCHOOLTEACHER took his children fishing. Nothing unusual about that. But this particular fisherman noticed that a high percentage of the fish he caught had visible tumors. Now, the fisherman's specialty was microbiology—he was Dr. Eric R. Brown, chairman of the microbiology department of Chicago Medical School.

Curious about the tumors, Dr. Brown initiated an investigation of the fish and of the water where he was fishing—Fox River, a typical American river flowing a few miles west of Chicago. The bacteria count ran as high as 39,000 per 100 milliliters of water. That indicated a high proportion of fecal matter. There were also herbicides, insecticides, phosphates, nitrates, gasoline, ether, and carcinogenic (cancer-producing) compounds of the benzanthracene group. In addition, there were lead, mercury, calcium, cadmium, zinc, and antimony.[1]

Fox River fish had a high incidence of cancers. Carp and suckers suffered the most—as high as 16 per cent. And carcinomas were the most common type; also, there were lymphosarcoma of the jaw, melanoma, and sarcoma of the gill area. Some fish had two or three types of solid tumor. (For comparison, a study was made of several Canadian rivers. These did not have nearly so much pollution, and the fish had fewer tumors.)

What a fish eats of elements such as mercury and arsenic, Dr. Brown points out, the fish keeps. When a bigger fish eats several smaller fish, he keeps the mercury and arsenic that they all ate. When a human being eats the fish, he keeps these poisons and they build up in him. This process of "biological magnification" is a major threat in the use of fish or animals as food.

Shellfish are grown in beds near where rivers empty into the sea. They live on the pollution brought by the rivers. And as mercury is a heavy element they get a lot of it. Recently there have been epidemics of mercury poisoning from shellfish in Japan and other areas.

Other elements that build up in the human body are compounds such as the polychlorinated biphenyl pesticides and chlorinated hydrocarbons. DDT, an example of the latter, has now been banned for certain purposes in some countries. But already there are several hundred million tons of it in the environment, and much is still being used. Experimentation with animals has demonstrated that DDT is carcinogenic and contributes to stillbirths.[2]

Because DDT is a stable molecule it does not degrade. It passes from plant to water, to fish, to insect, to bird, to animal, to man. Moreover, it accumulates in carnivores. The animal that eats the most other animals and is not likely to be eaten himself, is the most likely to accrete the most DDT and similar pesticides. That animal we describe as being at the top of the "food chain." And that "animal" is carnivorous man.

There is so much DDT already in the world's oceans it is inhibiting the growth of plankton, that tiny life form that is near the bottom of the food chain and is the basic food for many fish. Even around the Antarctic DDT has been found. PCB, another class of chemical used widely in industrial processes, has been found in practically all marine specimens, and usually in higher concentrations than DDT.[3]

Several herbicides, especially the one known as 2, 4, 5-T, have been demonstrated as "clearly teratogenic" (creating birth deformities) in laboratory mice. Yet millions of acres of land have been sprayed with this chemical since 1948. The President's science advisor, as well as the Surgeon General, has endorsed "limited action" against the use of this chemical. But it is still being used.

By now we probably cannot avoid getting some of these substances, even in a vegetarian diet. But the meat eater may eat in a few minutes the pesticides that an animal has collected over a lifetime. Meat, fish, and poultry contribute thirteen times the amount of DDT as the average amount in vegetables. Dairy products may have as much as one third that of meat.[4]

Some chemicals found in meat—antibiotics—were put there on purpose. More and more food animals are raised, not on open ranges, but in feed lots. This saves valuable land, keeps the animals from exercising away their weight gains, and makes forced feeding easier. But the crowded quarters add to the animals' stress, which increases the likeliness of disease. Also, in the feed lot once a disease starts it can spread faster. So antibiotics are added as a matter of course to the animal feed, as a prophylactic, for disease prevention. Some 80 per cent of U.S. food animals are raised on medicated feed.

Another purpose of the antibiotics is to make the meat keep longer once the animal has been slaughtered.

"There is always a spoilage problem with meat from the moment when the animal is killed. . . . The larger the animal, the greater the problem, but the basic principles involved in the spoilage of meat are the same whether one is dealing with whales, elephants, cattle, sheep or pigs."[5]

Antibiotics are used not only in large food animals. Aureomycin is used on fresh-caught fish to preserve it longer. (Present levels of usage aim to extend the shelf life of fish about one week.) Poultry are not only fed antibiotics—their carcasses are dipped into them in processing.[6]

Some people are allergic to antibiotics. Residues in meat, which cannot be cooked away, may cause nausea, vomiting, and diarrhea.[7]

But the greater problem with feeding antibiotics to food animals is genetical. Prolonged administration tends to allow certain strains of bacteria to develop that are immune to the drug and to similar drugs. That would offset the advantages of penicillin, tetracyclines, aureomycin, and others. Great Britain has already had at least one case where antibiotics in calves produced a drug-resistant salmonella strain that was transferred to farm workers, to dairy cattle, and into milk. In 1970 that country took steps to eliminate all antibiotics from animal feed.

Veterinarians recognize the potential danger of these antibiotics. One paper, for instance, while advocating the usage of antibiotics admits that,

"Poultry disease, enteric infections in pigs and calves, and mastitis in dairy cattle present a much greater problem today to both producers and public health officials than they did before the advent of the antibiotics."[8]

It seems evident, therefore, that the feeding of antibiotics to livestock is not the answer to the elimination and prevention of disease.

Ironically, the heavy use of antibiotics has not made the animals healthier.

"There has been no noticeable decrease in the incidence of disease of livestock and poultry that can be associated with the increased use of antibiotics in rations."[9]

Some of the additives in meat do not come under FDA jurisdiction. Take sodium nitrate and sodium nitrite, for example. These and similar compounds are used partly to preserve meat from spoiling and partly to maintain a reddish, healthy color. They are used largely in frankfurters, luncheon meats, and other processed meats. The FDA classifies both sodium nitrate and sodium nitrite as poisonous and deleterious substances. Yet they are allowed in meat—with no mention required on the label—because they were already in use before the Delaney Amendment (to the Food, Drug, and Cosmetics Act) became law in 1958.

Actually the preservative feature of nitrite plays the lesser role. If it were not for the cosmetic feature—to disguise spoiling meat—90 to 95 per cent of the chemical could be left out. Meanwhile, children have died from eating hot dogs that accidentally contained too high a level of nitrite.

The possibility has been raised that both nitrites and nitrates can be converted into substances called nitrosamines, by reaction to other chemicals in the foods and drugs taken into the body—articles such as cooked meat, beer, wine, tobacco, cereals, and certain medicines.[10] Certain of these nitrosamines are among the most potent cancer-producing agents known, and seem to be most effective in producing tumors when applied in small doses (as one would get in eating hot dogs) over a long period of time.[11] A noted toxicologist called nitrosamines "one of the major public health issues of our time."[12]

One of the most controversial elements in meat is that of the synthetic and other added hormones. Shortly after World War II cattlemen discovered that by administering estrogenic, or female, hormones to beef cattle their metabolism was altered. They gave more attention to eating and were able to put on more weight faster. An animal could mature in 15 months instead of two or three years. The extra meat kept retail prices lower, saving about $3.85 per person each year.

Today, synthetic hormones have been credited with adding some 25 per cent to the amount of beef available to the American consumer. Much of that is in water and fat, but that fact is not generally considered.[13]

What is being considered is that the hormones administered to food animals may cause cancer in the human beings who eat them. Take DES (diethylstilbestrol) for instance. This was a favorite hormone among beef raisers. But then it was noticed that among several daughters born to women who were treated with DES to prevent miscarriage, a disproportionate number developed vaginal cancer. Moreover, seventeen men who took DES as treatment for prostate cancer subsequently developed breast cancer—an otherwise rare disease among men.[14]

When DES produced cancer in laboratory mice, it was enough for the FDA to ban use of DES in treatment of human beings. The ban also included closely related chemicals such as dienestrol and promethestrol dipropionate.

Of course, attention soon turned to the use of DES in food animals. Some doctors pointed out that small dosages over a long period of time (such as one would get in eating meat containing DES residues) were more likely to produce cancer than larger doses over a short period of time.[15]

Three factors make the carcinogenic danger extremely insidious. One is the possible effect on fetuses. Animal embryos are extremely sensitive to carcinogens. Baby mice succumbed to dosages 1/4000th the size necessary to produce cancer in adult mice.[16] Is this same sensitivity present in human fetuses?

All these things are worrying those in a position to know what is at stake. In January, 1973, the United States Government restricted the use of DES in animals. (Ten other nations had already banned it, and Sweden and Italy would no longer import United States meat because of its DES.) Meat raisers promptly turned to other estrogenic hormones, for they were not ready, nor was the nation ready, to see the meat supply suddenly cut by as much as 25 per cent. Among the other substances they turned to were MGA (melengestrol acetate), which is fed to heifers (to reduce their interest in sex, so they will pay more attention to eating), and zeranol. In 1992 thousands of Puerto Rican children—some as young as 9 months—were found developing breasts and experiencing menstruation and stunted growth. They also had high levels of zeranol in their blood.

Ideally, any of these hormones is supposed to be discontinued a certain time before the animal is killed, with the hope there will be no residue in the meat. But how can the ideal be maintained on thousands of farms, manned not by veterinarians but by the farmers? There's no way to make sure MGA is not fed to steers, for instance. And who's going to guarantee the hormones are discontinued a certain number of days before the animals are brought to market? And who will police the amount fed by overzealous growers? To check the meat is a complicated laboratory process—only a relatively few carcasses can be examined each year.

Pig growers and poultry growers are not going to be left behind beef growers in technology. They have at their disposal similar hormones, and they are using them. Farmers inject pellets of estradiol monopalmitate into chicken necks. Dimetridazole is used with turkeys. Both have produced cancer in laboratories.

Reportedly, the USDA never intends to test for some of the hormones such as Synovex, because they are hormones that are also found naturally in the body—the "normal" amounts have not been determined. Now here's the rub: Hormones come close to the "secret of life," and scientists don't know enough about them to be able to tell why a little bit is good and too much is bad—or how much is too much.

That raises the specter, if artificially added hormones in meat spell too much hormones for the human body to handle, what about the hormones *naturally* occurring in meat? That question surfaced in the DES debate. Officials of FDA maintained DES was safe because it gets into meat in amounts far smaller than the natural estrogens produced by the human body and by cattle and sheep in heat. In other words, DES is less potent than natural hormones.[17] In any case we'd better be careful about upsetting our body chemistry by adding *any* hormones to our own. And certainly not day after day after day, without a doctor's prescription.

Of course, animals have been suffering from cancer all along, and many of those same animals find their way to the dinner table. Of course, it hasn't been *proved* that animal cancer can be transmitted to man. (The big obstacle is the length of time it takes a cancer to show.) But we know that some animal cancers can be transmitted to other animals (feline leukemia, for instance).[18] We know human cancer can be transmitted to animals. And it has not been proved that animal cancer *cannot* be transmitted to man.

Epidemiologically—that is, by looking at disease patterns among populations, as compared to clinical research studies—there is growing evidence that animal cancer does pass to human beings. Specialists say, for instance, that virtually all chickens harbor avian leukosis viruses, even though they may not show tumors. While farmers as a group have a low cancer mortality rate, chicken farmers run nearly six times the risk of dying of leukemia, over nonfarmers.[19]

D. Arnold Bendick, a molecular biologist at Michigan State University, expressed himself in a personal communication to Ralph Nader:

"We have no proof that avian leukosis-type viruses cannot cause cancer in man. Therefore, the spectre of long-term contact with the viruses is not encouraging. My professional opinion is that we have something to worry about."[20]

Cows contact leukemia, too, and there is similar epidemiological evidence of the transmissibility of bovine leukemia to humans.[21]

I'd like to leave the subject of cancer, but in frankness there is one more aspect that should be mentioned: Here's a family out in the back yard, preparing to enjoy an outdoor barbecue. Dad's got a funny white hat on, and Uncle Jim is helping him barbecue the steaks. Mom and Aunt Helen are making the salad. The steaks are sizzling on the racks; the fat is dripping out of the steaks and into the fire—the aroma is enough to make the mouth water.

But that fat dripping into the fire becomes superheated—to perhaps 1300°. The heat changes the chemical properties of the fat and produces, among other things, benzo(a)pyrene. Now, benzo(a)pyrene has long been established as one of the chief cancer-producing agents in tobacco smoke. Here in the charcoal grill that benzo(a)pyrene goes up in the smoke from the charcoal and coats the steaks.

Clinically run tests on charcoal-broiled steaks have shown

that each two-pound steak, well-done, contains an average of nine micrograms of benzo(a)pyrene—which works out to the equivalent of 600 cigarettes.[22] And that's too much for anybody.

DDT, PCB, DES, MGA—however you spell it, the additives that find their way into flesh foods spell trouble to the eater. Apparently logical reasons could be presented for using any or all of them, but surely the safest diet is the one that is the simplest and the closest to Mother Nature's own. Even vegetables may contain some pesticides, but only a fraction of what is contained in meat, and none of the antibiotics and hormones.

7

The Cholesterol Connection

ALL RIGHT, now suppose you have on your plate a piece of fresh steak, oven broiled, not charcoal broiled. And suppose that, not being satisfied with nominal USDA inspection, you have had this particular steak clinically examined and pronounced free of parasites, bacteria, and viruses. And you have the assurance the steak is free of added hormones (we'll just have to ignore the natural hormones for the present) and all toxic wastes have been washed out of it. Do you at last have a piece of good, nutritious food, ready to give energy and build body cells?

No, you're not yet home free. As with practically all flesh, the steak also has, as part and particle of its makeup, what cardiologists consider one of the "seven deadly sins"—saturated fat.

One of the main forms of heart and blood-vessel disease is arteriosclerosis—hardening of the arteries. Certain fatty substances tend to clog up the blood vessels, limiting the supply of blood to the various parts of the body. When the heart itself does not get a sufficient supply of blood to its muscles, portions will die.

There are several factors that lead to arteriosclerosis. Here are some of them, somewhat in order of their importance. The ones in parentheses are those we can't do much about:

(Heredity), diet, serum lipids, hypertension, stress, (age), obesity, (hormones), (vascular trauma), tobacco, (sex), physical activity, (liver function), (infection), (culture).[1] Serum lipids refer to the amount and make-up of fatty substances in the bloodstream, and are closely related to diet. Sex refers to the gender—males are more susceptible than females.

Notice that diet and serum lipids are high on the list of factors over which a person has control. Among these serum lipids are such things as cholesterol and triglycerides.

There is normally a predetermined amount of cholesterol in the human body. It is an important substance in bile acid, sex hormones, and adrenal hormones. But when it begins to build up in the arteries in combination with other fatty substances and threatens to close off the blood supply, look out.

Research strongly indicates that the cholesterol in the food we eat (dietary) increases the cholesterol in our blood (serum). Free cholesterol is found only in animal products. Brains have the most, and egg yolk is very high. Cheddar cheese has a medium amount, skim milk little or none.

One of the factors affecting cholesterol is the molecular make-up of fat, specifically saturated fat and polyunsaturated fat. When too much of the ingested fat is of the saturated type, the cholesterol level rises.

The fat in vegetables is high in polyunsaturated fatty acids and low in saturated fatty acids. We say the "p/s ratio" for vegetables is high—some have a ratio of 4 per cent. In animal products the opposite is true, and the ratio is low—beef has a ratio of .06. The lower the ratio, the greater the danger. In the United States, beef is the most guilty of all meats in providing saturated fat, thus raising the cholesterol level, and thus contributing to atherosclerosis.

Joliffe and Archer made a statistical study of the death rate from coronary heart disease in twenty countries. Of various dietary and environmental influences considered, consumption of saturated fats (mostly animal) and animal protein were the two most closely related factors. The greater the amount of animal fat and animal protein in relation to the total amount of food eaten, the greater was the incidence of coronary heart deaths.[2]

A joint statement of the Food and Nutrition Board (National Academy of Sciences—National Research Council) and the Council on Foods and Nutrition of the American Medical Association warns that the "average level of plasma lipids in most American men and women is undesirably elevated."[3] Further:

"In risk categories it is important to decrease substantially the intake of saturated fat and to lower cholesterol consumption. In practise, this entails substituting polyunsaturated vegetable oils for part of the saturated fat in the diet."[4]

This would mean, use skim milk instead of whole, soft margarine instead of butter, and go easy on eggs.

An interesting comparison between diets high in meat fats and one low in meat fats was provided in Korea. United States Army rations assayed at approximately 42 per cent fat. The Korean Army rations contained only about 15 per cent fat. Then for logistical reasons some of the Korean soldiers were fed United States Army rations. It was found that even after only a few weeks, the serum-lipid levels of the Koreans rose "significantly."[5]

A similar study among Japanese people in Japan, Hawaii, and the United States (thus with similar hereditary backgrounds but with different diets), noted that the closer they came to the American diet, the higher their incidence of heart disease.[6] Another study compared blacks in Uganda, East Africa, with blacks in St. Louis, U.S.A.[7]

Checking against these epidemiological studies, clinical trials have reached the same conclusions—that animal-fat diets contribute to a high cholesterol level in the blood serum, and a higher risk of heart and blood-vessel disease.[8] The evidence prompted an editorial statement in the *Journal of the American Medical Association* that a vegetarian diet can prevent 97 per cent of our coronary occlusions and 90 per cent of our thrombo-embolic disease.[9]

(While it does not come under the subject of heart disease or cholesterol, there is another plus to be gained from a vegetarian diet, in the area of bone health. A team compared bone density in lacto-ovovegetarians and omnivores. They noted a "significant difference" in the vegetarians and suggested they were less prone to osteoporosis [porous bone structure] than the omnivores. They also observed that osteoporosis continued to increase in omnivores as they grew older. But there was no increase in the vegetarians.[10]

This particular study did not give a reason for the difference. It suggested the higher degree of osteoporosis among omnivores might be due to the higher amount of acid ash in their diet, or because the vegetarian diet was higher in calcium, or to a combination of factors.)

The second most common cause of cancer death (after lung cancer) among U.S. men is cancer of the prostrate. In 1991, 32,000 died of it. A six-year study by Harvard University's School of Public Health (1993) found that those men who ate red meat as a main dish five or more times a week were two and a half times as likely to suffer advanced prostate cancer as men who ate red meat only once a week or less.[11] An earlier study indicated the same increase in incidence of colon cancer among women.[12]

The causal relationship of animal fats to heart and artery disease is probably the most clear-cut, immediate, and universal of all the drawbacks to the use of flesh as food. Parasites are not likely to survive in well-cooked meats. Hormones may not be added to feed. But the fat is always there, and always dangerous to health.

It is time now to consider the adequacy of a vegetarian diet, particularly whether it meets the protein requirements of the human body.

8

Vegetable Sources of Protein

NOW WE come to the crucial question—Can a person who does not eat meat expect to get as nutritious a diet as one who does? We're not interested in the word *substitute;* we're not looking for second-best. If, with all its drawbacks, flesh is still clearly what the body needs, we want to know it. But if we can have equally good or better nutrition, without the drawbacks of flesh, then we need to know that. And if at the same time we can save money, who will complain?

First, we might ask, why do people eat meat? The most obvious reason is, it is food. All right, we will get to that. Another reason, through the centuries it has always been the wealthier people who could afford to eat meat, just as they were the ones to ride in fine carriages and live in big houses. So, public opinion plays a part. We like to consider ourselves as "successful" as others. But that is a false standard, and has often led people astray, morally, politically, and nutritionally. Of course, people like the flavor of meat. But that is an acquired taste and really has no part in whether it is good for us.

Two "scientific" theorems, based on fallacies, have encouraged the demand for meat. In the mid-nineteenth century a man named Liebig declared that protein was the body's source of energy to perform work. The assumption followed that we must eat a lot of protein. Now we know that the body gets its energy largely from fats and carbohydrates. Some protein is converted into carbohydrates, but in the main protein is needed for growth and for replacing the cells that are constantly wearing out in the body. Protein also plays a role in regulating body chemistry—salt and water balances, and the acid-base balance of blood. Protein requirements are constant and not increased significantly by physical activity.

Amplifying Liebig's error, Voit, a German physiologist and a contemporary of Liebig, recommended that the body needed 118 grams of protein every day. But Voit based his recommendation, not on what the hefty Germans *needed,* but on what they were actually *eating.* Today the National Research Council recommends approximately 65 grams of protein for men and 55 grams for women every day. But even these are generous amounts, leaving plenty of margin. Under normal circumstances 30 to 35 grams is enough for men and some sources say 25.[1] (Children and pregnant women need more.)

We also know the protein cannot be stored by the body, like fat, against a rainy day. What is not used for body building is changed into carbohydrates and used as energy or passed out of the body. There is even a possibility of too high a protein intake. The liver and kidneys are the organs called upon to change excess protein, and too much work puts a strain on them. Because of this extra work the body heat level is raised and the fluid balance is upset.[2] A continued excess may result in damage to the kidneys.[3]

Years ago Russell Henry Chittenden, a physiological chemist at Yale University, stated a concept that is still held and often quoted: The smallest amount of food able to keep the body in a state of high efficiency is physiologically the most economical, and thus best adapted for the body's needs.[4] Too little food is bad, but so is too much. The average American diet contains 45 per cent more protein than the National Academy of Sciences recommends,[5] therefore to that extent it is not "best adapted for the body's needs."

There are three major differences between vegetarian protein and protein of animal origin. First, there is production. Vegetarian sources are much more efficient, by about ten to one, as has already been shown (Chapter 2). Moreover, vegetarian protein is more easily stored and transported, with not nearly so much danger of spoilage, contamination, or disease.

Second, vegetarian proteins are not so concentrated as animal proteins. This is a minus in the sense that you have to take more mouthfuls in order to get your requirements, but it is a plus in that foods that are too concentrated, without enough roughage, may lead to constipation and, according to some authorities, may contribute to cancer of the colon. Many a meat eater upon switching to a vegetarian diet has found his constipation clearing up without the use of laxatives.

The third difference, the one most important to our discussion and the one we will spend the most time on, is the respective biological values of the proteins available from the two sources.

There are many different kinds of proteins, built on different formulas. Of the kind the human body is made of, meat, milk, and eggs come the closest to matching. That is because animals are closer to man's make-up than are plants. But we don't have to eat the animals to get the proteins, anymore than do pigs, whose physiological requirements are quite similar to man's. They get along very well on vegetarian diets, and so can man.

The human body does not absorb protein as such, anyway. Protein in any form—plant, animal, or human—is made up of varying formulas of its "building blocks," the amino acids. The human body has to take protein, animal or vegetable, and break it down in the digestive process into these basic units and then build its own proteins from them. There are more than a million kinds of protein used in the body—one kind for red blood cells, another kind for fingernails, another for glands, et cetera.

There are twenty or more amino acids that the body needs, in varying amounts. Most of them the human body can synthesize from carbohydrates and fats. But there are eight or so that it should have regularly in the diet. These eight, called essential amino acids, are isoleucine, leucine, lysine, methionine, phenylalanine, threonine, tryptophan, and valine. Infants need, in addition, histidine. A complete protein food is one that includes all eight of these essential acids in more or less the right proportions for body use in digestible form.

As mentioned, meats, eggs, and milk proteins most nearly match the body's needs for the essential amino acids. But none of these is a complete food, for other nutrients are needed besides protein. For example, meat is the poorest source of magnesium. Plants provide, on the average, more than twice the amount of vitamins and minerals found in meat and fish. Riboflavin and calcium are best obtained from milk and eggs rather than from meat.

The fact is, plants are an excellent source of protein, also. Cereals are about 10 per cent protein, beans are about 25 per cent, and soybeans are as much as 40 per cent protein. Soybeans have twice as much protein as cheese, twice as much as red meat, and ten times as much as milk. Moreover, soybeans contain all eight of the essential amino acids—in fact, a higher quantity of all amino acids (weight for weight) than meat or eggs.[6] Soybeans also contain calcium, phosphorus, iron, and more of the B vitamins, thiamine and riboflavin, than meat, and more niacin than eggs (but less niacin than meat).

But while plants have a lot of protein, it was once felt that their protein was not as usable by the body as animal protein. This idea was supported by a study of the feeding of laboratory rats.

But those studies were based on feeding *single* plant proteins as compared with meat proteins. Now it is known that a *variety* of plants *supplement* one another, and supply more than enough usable protein. What one type of plant will lack in the way of an essential amino acid another plant will supply. Beans and rice, for instance, as enjoyed in Latin America, make an excellent protein combination. Or corn and beans, as in

Mexico, or soybeans and cottonseed protein. Wheat with milk is another good combination.

Generally speaking, grains and legumes make a good protein combination, or grains and dairy products, or legumes and seeds. A combination of lentils and wheat gluten produced growth in clinical tests as satisfactory as condensed milk.[7] Other combinations are helpful but not so complete as these. From this it may be seen the vegetarian diet can be widely varied in flavor, texture, color, and every appeal.

When amino acids were first studied, it was thought that to make up a complete protein, all eight of the essential acids must be eaten at the same meal. But now it is understood that the body can make up temporary deficiencies from the pool of materials within the body system—the materials supplied as old cells break down, from materials sloughed off intestinal walls, digestive secretions, et cetera.[8] Some people, beside refraining from using meat, may not wish to use dairy products. The main problem here is the need for vitamin B_{12}. There is no presently known practical source for this vitamin in plant foods.

A lack of vitamin B_{12} in the diet may eventually manifest itself in certain individuals. Some may experience pernicious anemia. A few may suffer, after ten or fifteen years, the deterioration of certain nerve fibers. On the other hand, many seem to do well for years without this vitamin, with no observable or even clinical evidence of damage.[9]

Calcium is not a great problem, even in a diet that does not include milk, if there is enough intake of green, leafy vegetables. However, children, who cannot digest greens properly, need milk for calcium.

Some may fear to use dairy products because of cholesterol. Whole milk has only a fraction the cholesterol that meat has (22 mg per 100 grams, as compared to 70 mg for beef, or 90 mg for veal). Further, one can gain the necessary vitamin B_{12}, calcium, protein, and vitamin D from low-fat dairy products. These would also be lower in pesticides and hormone residues than whole milk, because these substances are stored in the fat or cream.

"A vegetarian diet supplemented by fairly liberal amounts of milk is the most satisfactory type of diet that man can take."[10]

So much for the theory. How well does it work out in practice? Mention has already been made of the state of health of the Hunzas of northern Pakistan, of vegetarian tribes of India, et cetera. During World War I, Denmark was faced with a severe food shortage because of an Allied blockade of the coast. By government order most of the food animals were slaughtered. Without these mouths to feed, the cereal and vegetable supply was sufficient for the people. At the end of the war the Danes discovered their incidence of deaths had been reduced by 2.1 per thousand, lower than ever before. Their meatless diet was given the credit. As they resumed their prewar diet of meat, however, the death rate went up again.[11]

Right after World War II, the nutritional condition of thousands of Europeans was reported. Although 95 to 100 per cent of their protein had come from grains and potatoes, few of the people showed clinical or laboratory evidence of protein deficiency. Even those who did have such symptoms improved when they got enough of the same food they had been eating. In other words, theirs was not so much a protein deficiency as a calorie deficiency.[12]

Many studies have been made of many diets—different countries, different customs, different foods available. Some studies of some vegetarians have not reflected favorably on their diet—usually because it was too restricted, either from religious scruples or simply a lack of quantity or variety of food. *No* study of lacto-ovo-vegetarians, who have had a reasonable variety of cereals and legumes, in addition to leafy vegetables, has ever shown them to disadvantage in growth or energy as compared to nonvegetarians.

A vegetable protein mixture, supplied as a relief item, was found effective among war victims after World War II. With that experience at hand, nutritionists went to work to find an inexpensive source of protein to feed the millions of undernourished children of Central and South America. They came up with Incaparina, a high-protein powder consisting of corn meal, sorghum, cottonseed flour, torula yeast (a by-product of papermill waste), Vitamin A, and calcium carbonate (obtained for this project from slaked lime). Most of the ingredients were indigenous to the countries needing the aid. The mixture could provide a day's requirements of protein for one child for four cents.[13]

Severe cases of protein deficiency, including kwashiorkor, have been successfully treated with such plant protein mixtures.[14]

In a well-documented study, Drs. Mervyn Hardinge and Frederick Stare compared the diets and respective states of health of two hundred Americans. The group under study comprised 112 vegetarians (including some pure vegetarians) and 88 nonvegetarians—men and women, boys and girls. There were pregnant women representing both types of diets.

In regard to growth characteristics, the following observation was made by the researchers:

"The non-vegetarian adolescents consumed significantly more protein than did the lacto-ovo-vegetarian adolescents; however, this larger protein intake was not reflected in greater growth as measured by height."[15]

Expectant mothers will be interested also in the following conclusions:

"No evidence was obtained to indicate that a lacto-ovo-vegetarian diet failed to provide the dietary standards recommended for adequate nutrition for an expectant mother.

"The average birth weights and birth lengths of the two groups of infants were not statistically different."[16]

Preconception and postpartum weight gains and losses were similar as well.

*Average Protein Intake**	Grams of Protein a Day Man	Woman
Recommended Daily Allowance	65g	55g
Vegetarian	83	61
Lacto-ovo-vegetarian	98	82
Nonvegetarian	125	94

* Hardinge, Mervyn G., and Frederick J. Stare, "Nutritional Studies of Vegetarians: 1. Nutritional, Physical, and Laboratory Studies," *Journal of Clinical Nutrition,* 2:73, 1954, p. 76.

As for the adults, men and women, the study found there was no significant association between the blood pressure and a vegetable diet. There was no lowering of serum protein values—even among those who had been "pure" vegetarians for ten or fifteen years. In fact, the total protein, albumin, and globulin values, and all hematological findings, for all vegetarian and nonvegetarian groups were not statistically different.

In regard to amino acid intake, the diet of the pure vegetarians closely resembled the pattern of proteins of human milk. It was a little low in lysine, but still higher than that stipulated by the Food and Agriculture Organization of the United Nations as minimum. The diet of lacto-ovo-vegetarians as well as that of nonvegetarians was similar to the amino acid pattern of cow's milk. In fact, the amino acid intake for all three groups ranged from twice to many times the minimum essential amino acid requirements. (While minimum standards have been set, the optimum levels have not been established.)

In an even more thorough-going and clinically controlled study, the nitrogen intake of a group of young adults was compared with the nitrogen excreted. (Nitrogen is a readily measured index to the amount of protein actually absorbed by the body.) The three groups, vegetarian, lactovegetarian, and nonvegetarian, were fed each according to his respective diet, but carefully measured as to nitrogen content (10-g per day). Results: There was no significant difference in the ability of the three diets tested to maintain the nitrogen balance.

So there we have the picture from a medical and nutritional

viewpoint—when a person eats a variety of wholesome foods, he or she does not need meat to grow, to produce children, to work, to maintain robust health.

It would be well to emphasize the phrase, "variety of wholesome foods." This includes whole-grain cereals—whole-wheat bread, whole-wheat or oat or corn breakfast cereals. (Many modern women are making their own whole-wheat bread.) Whole potatoes and carrots, and other vegetables, as far as possible. Orange juice, not simply sweetened orange "drink."

A person can get "full" on refined white flour and sugar. But there is something missing in the nutrition there—that is why they are called empty calories. Much of the nutrition has been refined away. Even enriched bread is lacking, because the roughage of the bran in whole-wheat bread is also needed by the intestines for normal peristalsis.

The beauty of a diet based on a variety of wholesome foods is that one food complements another. No single food has all the nutrition, the protein, the carbohydrates, the minerals, the vitamins, the bulk and roughage, that the body needs. And here is the danger in fad diets, such as cottage cheese, carrot juice, grape juice, et cetera. These are good substances, but not good enough alone. The same is true of the Zen macrobiotic diet. Brown rice is better than polished rice, but it surely is not enough by itself.

How do vegetarians rate beside meat eaters in athletic competition? The answer to that is, Very well, thank you. Considering their relative numbers in population, vegetarians have exceeded meat eaters, especially in endurance tests. There have been several Olympic champions in running events who were vegetarians, and vegetarians usually walk away with the honors in walking competitions (a popular British competition). Murray Rose, hailed as "the best all-rounder Australia has ever produced," won two gold medals in the 1956 Olympic swimming contests (he won the 1500 meters free style and set on Olympic record for 400 meters). And he did it as a vegetarian.

Bicycle ergometer tests were run on subjects in Stockholm, comparing the endurance based on all-meat diets, mixed diets, and high-carbohydrate diets (without meat). The latter provided 50 per cent more energy than the second, and about three times more than the first.[17]

In more recent history, there is Ralph (Chip) Oliver, former linebacker for the Oakland Raiders, who told his story in *Sports Illustrated.*[18] He says, "I wouldn't get tired. I was feeling stronger in the fourth quarter than in the first. I improved my range and my quickness and my strength." Chip finally quit the game in disgust and protest over his teammates' habits of "belching beefsteak and downing bennies."

Then there is Anders Haugen, perennial ski champion—at 84 years old he's still skiing! He won national championships, and set a world record for a ski jump he made in Colorado. He captained the first American ski team to the Olympics—they beat the Norwegians—and was subsequently elected to the Hall of Fame. Anders has been a vegetarian for sixty years.

So you can see what I mean when I say vegetarians are not on the defensive about their diet. They are not martyrs, who have "given up" meat. No, they have made a reasonable decision on the basis of the evidence. They have made a rational choice to use for food only that which has proved to be best for their bodies.

In the last chapter you will find some suggestions in making a changeover from a flesh to a vegetarian dietary.

9

Going Vegetarian

SO NOW you are ready to give the vegetarian diet at least a try. You could do worse. But you would also be well-advised not to do anything drastic. You yourself probably could do all right—after all, you've read this book! But others in your family might have some reaction, at least psychologically. And this is not a fad you're taking up, a come-again, gone-again, fly-by-night sort of thing. You want to build sensibly.

You can begin by discarding pork and all hog products. Those are among the worst offenders, with their fat and possible parasites, and you don't need them: frankfurters, bacon, luncheon meat, sausage, lard, hamburgers. Use only lean beef or lamb. Be sure to cook the meat well done, in or on a stove (not on a grill).

Meat is stimulating—all those hormones in the system. You would miss it, perhaps have a "let-down" feeling, if you cut it all out at once. So taper off—have some once a day for a few days, then every other day, then once a week. In the meantime, you build up your intake of legumes and whole-grain cereals. Now you can strike out on your new life. And you may well feel a new life. Many have experienced a lightness, a *joie de vivre,* in returning to a diet based on "living food" rather than flesh.

The Basic Four food categories are popularly classified as (1) fruits and vegetables, (2) meat, eggs, and other high-protein foods, (3) cereals and grains, (4) dairy products. To adapt this to a lacto-ovo-vegetarian diet (vegetarian plus milk and eggs) is relatively simple: Cut down on sweets and white-flour products, use more milk products, and use legumes, whole-grain cereals, and nuts instead of meat.

Milk products could well be limited to those of the nonfat or low-fat variety, such as cottage cheese. Eggs should not exceed one a day—two or three a week would probably be enough. If you use cheese, stick with the unaged, process cheeses. Soft margarine, especially the kind made with corn oil, contains no cholesterol; butter is high in it.

There are some people who want to cut out milk as well, or are allergic to it. They will find fortified soymilk (usually sold in powder form, to be mixed with water) quite tasty, well tolerated, and nonallergenic. It permits normal growth in children, even in those who have failed to grow on other diets. Green leafy vegetables must be eaten regularly—at least one serving every day—to supply calcium, niacin, riboflavin. Vitamin B_{12} may be taken in tablet form if desired or necessary.

Children may find it difficult to develop a liking for vegetables and fruit, especially if they have not been served much in the past. Studies show that those families who grow their own food have the widest acceptance of that food. But, of course, not everyone can grow their own food. Fussy eaters usually come from permissive homes; open eaters are from homes where parents encourage their children to at least try a mouthful of each food. See that the food is as fresh as possible, and not overcooked or all mixed together on the plate. Serve seldom-used vegetables occasionally, and explore new ways of preparing and serving food, giving attention to color as well as texture.

A little time in developing a good recipe file will provide a wide variety of dishes that will please any palate. We are providing a list of recipe books that are worth the investment. If you cannot find them in your bookstore, simply write a letter to the respective publishers and they will gladly help you.

Consider now the ways a vegetarian diet is better:

1. It conserves food for a hungry world.
2. It is free from parasites and most food-poisoning microbes.
3. It is free from animal disease, such as tuberculosis and cancer.
4. It makes for stronger bones.
5. It supplies plenty of protein without being in wasteful excess.
6. It is free from hormones, antibiotics, and much of the pesticides that are in meat.
7. It does not require the slaughter of other creatures.
8. It is conducive to healthy arteries.
9. It is more economical.
10. It is more likely to supply sufficient vitamins and minerals.

Join the millions of Americans and others around the world who have learned how to eat healthfully!

References

Chapter 1

[1] Ellen G. White, *Counsels on Diet and Foods* (Washington, D.C.: Review and Herald Publishing Association, 1938), p. 390.

Chapter 2

[1] Charles F. Wurster, "DDT reduces Photosynthesis by Marine Phytoplankton," *Science,* 158: 1474-1475, 1968.

[2] *The World Food Problem* (The President's Science Advisory Committee, 1967), vol. 1, p. 14.

[3] Aaron M. Altschul, *Proteins: Their Chemistry and Politics* (New York: Basic Books, 1965), p. 264.

[4] L. H. Bean, cited in *The World Food Problem,* vol. 2, p. 336.

[5] *The World Food Problem,* vol. 2, p. 336.

[6] Frances Moore Lappé, *Diet for a Small Planet* (New York: Ballantine, 1971), pp. 8, 9.

[7] *Feed Situation,* August, 1969, p. 21.

[8] Lyle P. Schertz, *War on Hunger,* vol. 5, No. 6, June, 1971, p. 12.

[9] Altschul, *loc. cit.*

[10] *The World Food Problem,* vol. 2, pp. 331, 332.

[11] Aaron M. Altschul, "Combating Malnutrition: New Strategies Through Food Science," *Plant Foods for Human Nutrition,* vol. 1, No. 3 (1969), p. 152.

[12] Harrison Wellford, *Sowing the Wind* [a Nader Report] (New York: Grossman Publishers, 1971, 1972), p. 110.

[13] W. S. Collens and G. B. Dobkin, "Phylogenetic Aspects of the Cause of Human Atherosclerotic Disease" [abstract], Supplement II to *Circulation,* vols. 31 and 32 (October, 1965), p. II-7, by permission of the American Heart Association, Inc.

[14] O. Schloss, cited by Mervyn G. Hardinge and Hulda Crooks, "Non-Flesh Dietaries, II, Scientific Literature," *Journal of the American Dietetic Association,* 43:551, December, 1963.

Chapter 3

[1] L. M. Bernstein, *Renal Function and Renal Failure* (Baltimore: The Williams and Wilkins Company, 1965), p. 31.

[2] *Ibid.,* p. 28.

[3] Wellford, *Sowing the Wind,* pp. 129, 130.

[4] *Federal Register,* Oct. 3, 1970, pp. 15,600, 15,601.

Chapter 4

[1] Wellford, *Sowing the Wind,* The Washington *Post,* July 4, 1994.

[2] A. N. Wilder and R. A. MacCready, *New England Journal of Medicine,* vol. 274, No. 26, June 30, 1966, p. 1457.

[3] *Ibid.*

[4] *Wholesome Poultry Products Act,* hearings, Committee on Agriculture and Forestry, U.S. Senate, July 2, 1968, p. 279. Cited by Wellford, *op. cit.,* pp. 133, 134.

[5] The Washington *Post,* Dec. 10, 1994.

[6] H. Pivnick, *et al.,* "Staphylococcus Food Poisoning From Barbecued Chicken," *Canadian Journal of Public Health,* January, 1968, p. 31.

[7] Thomas L. Bott, *et al.,* "Clostridium Botulinum Type E in Fish From the Great Lakes,"

Journal of Bacteriology, vol. 91 (1966), 922.

[8] J. R. Chipley and K. N. May, "Survival of Aerobic and Anaerobic Bacteria in Chicken Meat During Freeze-Dehydration, Rehydration, and Storage," *Applied Microbiology,* vol. 16, March 1968, p. 448.

[9] P. Beeson and Walsh McDermott, eds., A *Textbook of Medicine* (Philadelphia: W. B. Saunders Company, 1971), p. 381.

[10] W. M. Henderson and J. B. Brooksby, "The Survival of Foot-and-Mouth Disease Virus in Meat and Offal," *Journal of Hygiene,* 46:394-402, 1948.

[11] G. E. Cottral, *et al.,* "The Survival of Foot-and-Mouth Disease Virus in Cured and Uncured Meats," *American Journal of Veterinary Medicine,* March 1960, pp. 288 ff.

[12] Dr. W. L. Ingalls, cited in Wellford, *op. cit.,* p. 2.

[13] *Ibid.*

[14] Beeson, *op. cit.,* pp. 736, 737.

[15] Don A. Schanche, "Bad News for Cat Lovers," *Family Health,* October, 1971, p. 16.

[16] *Ibid.*

[17] Beeson, *op. cit.*

Chapter 5

[1] Wellford, *Sowing the Wind,* pp. 12-16, 73, 74.

[2] The Washington *Post,* Nov. 17, 1971.

[3] *Ibid.,* May 28, 1993.

[4] Wellford, *op. cit.,* p. 46.

[5] Oscar Sussman, "Does the Wholesome Meat Act of 1967 Really Protect the Consumer?" *Veterinary Medicine,* 63:639, July 1968.

[6] Wellford, *op. cit.,* pp. 80-85.

[7] *Ibid.,* pp. 90-94.

[8] *Ibid.,* p. 137.

[9] *Ibid.,* p. 139.

[10] The Washington [D.C.] *Evening Star-Daily News,* June 28, 1973.

[11] Wellford, *op. cit.,* p. 150.

[12] *Lappé, Diet for a Small Planet,* p. 24.

[13] The Washington [D.C.] *Sunday Star,* Oct. 3, 1971.

[14] *Journal of the American Medical Association,* July 6, 1957.

[15] Adeline Thomas, "What Meat Buyers Should Know," *Review and Herald,* March 14, 1968, p. 8.

[16] "A Close Look at Hamburger," *Consumer Reports,* August 1971, p. 479.

[17] Wellford, *op. cit.,* pp. 68, 69.

[18] A Close Look at Hamburger," *Consumer Reports,* August 1971, p. 479.

[19] Ibid.

Chapter 6

[1] "The Fish Have Cancer. Is the Water Drinkable?" *Medical World News,* June 23, 1971, p. 80.

[2] Wellford, *Sowing the Wind,* p. 332.

[3] National Science Foundation, in The Washington [D.C.] *Evening Star,* Oct. 30, 1971.

[4] Lappé, *op. cit.,* p. 20.

[5] Ella M. Barnes, "The Use of Antibiotics for the Preservation of Poultry and Meat," *Nutritio et Dieta,* vol. 10 (1968), pp. 65, 66.

[6] *Ibid.,* p. 64.

[7] Lynn Rinehart, "What's Wrong With Meat?" *Fitness for Living,* May-June 1972, p. 68.

[8] C. K. Whitehair and B. S. Pomeroy, "Veterinary Medical Basis for the Use of Antibiotics

in Feeds," *The Use of Drugs in Animal Feeds* (National Academy of Sciences, Publication 1679, 1969), pp. 50, 51.

[9] *Ibid.*

[10] William Lijinsky and Samuel Epstein, "Nitrosamines as Environomental Carcinogens, *Nature,* 225:5227 (Jan. 3, 1970).

[11] Statement of Dr. William Lijinsky, University of Nebraska, before the Intergovernmental Relations Subcommittee, of the Committee on Government Operations, U.S. House of Representatives, March 16, 1971.

[12] Dr. Samuel Epstein, cited by Ralph Nader, "Don't Eat That Dog," *The New Republic,* April 18, 1972, p. 13.

[13] "Rearing Practice and Beef Quality," *Nutrition Reviews,* vol. 26, No. 10 (October 1968), p. 311.

[14] The Washington *Post,* Oct. 29, 1971.

[15] Harold G. Petering, "Foods and Feeds as Sources of Carcinogenic Factors," *Nutrition Reviews,* vol. 24, No. 11 (November 1966), P. 323.

[16] *Ibid.,* Nov. 11, 1971.

[17] The Washington *Post,* Feb. 14, 1972.

[18] *Ibid.,* Aug. 15, 1973.

[19] "What Causes Cancer on the Farm?" *Medical World News,* Jan. 14, 1972.

[20] D. Arnold Bendick, Michigan State University, to Ralph Nader. Cited by Wellford, *op. cit.,* p. 84.

[21] Anna Wolska, "Human and Bovine Leukaemias," *The Lancet,* May 25, 1968.

[22] William Lijinsky and P. Shubick, "Benzo(a)pyrene in Charcoal-Broiled Meat," *Science,* vol. 145 (July 3, 1964), p. 53.

Chapter 7

[1] Grace A. Goldsmith, *Journal of the American Medical Association,* 176:783 (June 3, 1961).

[2] N. Jolliffe and M. Archer, "Statistical Associations Between International Coronary Heart Disease Death Rates and Certain Environmental Factors," *Journal of Chronic Diseases,* vol. 9, No. 6 (June 1959), pp. 636-652.

[3] J. M. R. Beveridge, *et al.,* "Dietary Factors Affecting the Level of Plasma Cholesterol in Humans. The Role of Fat," *Canadian Journal of Biochemistry and Physiology,* vol. 34 (1956), p. 447.

[4] "Diet and Coronary Heart Disease," *Nutrition Review,* vol. 30 (October 1972), p. 244.

[5] Kyu Taik Lee, *et al.,* "Chemicopathologic Studies in Geographic Pathology," *Archives of Internal Medicine,* vol. 109, No. 4 (April 1962), pp. 98-104.

[6] Tavia Gordon, "Mortality Experience Among the Japanese in the United States, Hawaii and Japan," *Public Health Reports,* vol. 72, No. 6 (June 1957), p. 551.

[7] W. A. Thomas, *et al,* "Incidence of Myocardial Infarction Correlated With Venous and Pulmonary Thrombosis and Embolism: Geographic Study Based on Autopsies in Uganda, East Africa, and St. Louis, U.S.A.," *American Journal of Cardiology,* vol. 5 (January 1960), pp. 41-47.

[8] Seymour Dayton, "Diet High in Unsaturated Fat," *Minnesota Medicine,* August 1969, pp. 1237 ff. Also, Georgiana Walker, *et al.,* "The Effect of Animal Protein and Vegetarian Protein Diets Having the Same Fat Content on the Serum Lipid Levels of Young Women," *Nutrition,* vol. 72, No. 60, pp. 317-321.

[9] *Journal of the American Medical Association,* June 3, 1961, p. 806.

[10] Frey R. Ellis, *et al.,* "Incidence of Osteoporosis in Vegetarians and Omnivores," *American Journal of Clinical Nutrition,* vol. 25, No. 6 (June 6, 1972), pp. 555-558.

[11] The Washington *Post,* Oct. 6, 1993.

[12] *Ibid.,* Dec. 13, 1990.

Chapter 8

[1] Ancel Keys, "Caloric Undernutrition and Starvation," *Journal of the American Medical Association,* vol. 138, No. 7 (1948), p. 503; D. M. Hegsted, *et al.,* (Protein Requirements of Adults," *Journal of Laboratory and Clinical Medicine,* vol. 31 (1946), p. 261.

[2] Margaret Doyle, *et al,* "Observations on Nitrogen and Energy Balance in Young Men Consuming Vegetarian Diets," *American Journal of Clinical Nutrition,* vol. 17 (December 1965).

[3] Newton Evans and E. H. Riley, "High Protein Ration as a Cause of Nephritis," *California and Western Medicine,* April 1925.

[4] R. H. Chittenden, cited by Mervyn Hardinge and Hulda Crooks, "Non-Flesh Dietaries, II. Scientific Literature," *Journal of the American Dietetic Association,* vol. 43, No. 6 (December 1963), p. 551.

[5] *The World Food Problem,* p. 317.

[6] *Amino Acid Content of Food* (Home Economics Report No. 4, United States Department of Agriculture).

[7] *Journal of Nutrition,* 38:222, 1949.

[8] *Journal of the American Medical Association,* May 11, 1957, p. 176.

[9] G. A. Dhopeshwarkar, *et al.,* "The Effect of Vegetarianism and Antibiotics Upon Proteins and Vitamin B_{12} in the Blood," *The British Journal of Nutrition,* vol. 10, No. 2 (1956).

[10] Arturi I. Virtanen, *Federation Proceedings,* vol. 27, No. 6 (1968), p. 1376.

[11] M. Hindhede, "The Effect of Food Restriction During War on Mortality in Copenhagen," *Journal of the American Medical Association,* vol. 74, No. 6 (1920), p. 381.

[12] D. M. Hegsted, *et al.,* (Protein Requirements of Adults," *Journal of Laboratory and Clinical Medicine,* vol. 31 (1946), p. 261.

[13] Harland Manchester, "New Food for Hungry Children," *Reader's Digest,* September, 1963, pp. 137-141.

[14] N. S. Scrimshaw and R. Bressani, "Vegetable Protein Mixtures for Human Consumption," *Federation Proceedings,* vol. 20, Part III Supplement (1961), p. 80.

[15] Mervyn G. Hardinge and Frederick J. Stare, "Nutritional Studies of Vegetarians," I, *The Journal of Clinical Nutrition,* vol. 2, No. 2 (March-April, 1954), p. 80.

[16] *Ibid.,* p. 77.

17 Per-Olaf Astrand, "Something Old, Something New . . . Very New," *Nutrition Today,* vol. 3, No. 2 (June 1968), pp. 9-11.

18 Blaine Newnham, "Wow, Like Let's Really Try to Win," *Sports Illustrated,* Oct. 12, 1970,. pp. 50-52.

Recommended Recipe Books

The following books of vegetarian recipes may be obtained from ABC Mailing Service, Box 1119, Hagerstown, Maryland 21741:

Choices: Quick and Easy Cooking
Presents the natural goodness of fruits, vegetables, nuts, legumes, and grains to form delicious meals you can create in 30 minutes or less. Meets the dietary guidelines of the American Heart Association.

Fabulous Food for Family and Friends
An attractive collection of healthy, mouth-watering recipes for entertaining.

I Can't Believe It's Not Fattening
More than 100 recipes and brief suggestions that will tickle your taste buds and help you to a new lifestyle.

It's Your World Vegetarian Cookbook
The ultimate in cookbooks for those who want to know scientific details of the many facets of vegetarian cookery. More than 500 recipes.

Quick and Easy Cooking
In addition to vegetarian recipes low in cholesterol, saturated fats, salt, and sugar, this book includes 25 complete and nutritionally balanced menus.

CW01652478

TO

JESSICA

LOVE FROM

....

Jessica has a pet unlike any other. He doesn't have whiskers, or fur, or cute fluffy ears.

He doesn't fetch sticks in the park, or chase his tail, and he can't curl up in Jessica's lap for a snooze.

But he does have three LITTLE toes.

And a L-O-N-G neck.

And an even L-O-N-G-E-R tail.

And that's because Jessica's pet is a dinosaur.

Called Dexter.

Although Dexter can't meow, or bark, or squeak, or moo, or quack, he does have a great big roar. Just not today.

"It's ... gone," whispered Dexter. "Yesterday I was roaring loads, but now there's nothing. Not even a growl."

"It can't have vanished completely," said Jessica. "We'll just have to look for it. Come on, let's go!"

And so their great roar hunt began....

First, Jessica and Dexter searched the park. As they walked around, Jessica thought she could hear something. Could it really be Dexter's roar?

OOMPAH! OOMPAH! OOMPAH!

"That's not my roar, that's a brass band!" said Dexter.

"Carry on walking down the road," said the band leader. "I'm sure I heard something earlier today that could have been a roar."

"Thanks!" said Jessica. "Let's go, Dexter!"

TOOOOT
POM POM POM

Suddenly, Jessica and Dexter heard a booming sound that got louder and louder.

But the closer and closer they got, the less and less it sounded like a roar.

BOOM! BOOM! BOOM!

Jessica turned to Dexter: "That's not ..."

"... my roar," frowned Dexter.

"Ha! My wrecking ball's never been mistaken for a dinosaur roar before," chuckled the crane driver. "Try the beach, there's always strange noises coming from there."

"Phew," said Jessica. "All this roar hunting is tiring work. Come on, let's get an ice cream."

As Jessica and Dexter wandered across the sand they heard a distant sound getting closer.

"Uh-oh, what's that?" said Dexter.

SQUAWK! SQUAWK! SQUAWK!

"Aaahh! Seagulls!" shouted Jessica. "They're after the ice cream! Time for more roar hunting!"

FIRE

They ran and ran and ran until they could run no more.

Suddenly, Dexter spotted something big, red and shiny coming towards them. It was their friendly neighbourhood firefighters.

"Hey, our siren can make a noise as big as a roar," they said. "Will that do?"

NEE-NAW! NEE-NAW! NEE-NAW!

"Hmm, it's kind of close, but it's still not really a roar," said Jessica.

"It's a nee-no from me," said Dexter.

"Why don't you try asking a vet why your roar's disappeared?" said the firefighters. "We'll take you to see our friend – hop in!"

"I've never ever examined a dinosaur before," said the vet.
"Oh well, here goes!"

"AAAHHH," said Dexter as she looked down his throat.

"EEEEK," said Dexter as she looked in his ears.

"WAA, that tickles," said Dexter as she examined his tummy.

"Well, this is strange, I can't see anything," puzzled the vet. "Why don't you go to the school library and hunt for your roar there?"

BRRRRIIINNGGG
SCHOOL

Jessica spotted her best friend's brother in the playground.

"Dinosaur books?" he said. "Yes, there's loads in the library. Go in the main door and just follow the signs."

"Come on, Dexter, let's go!" said Jessica.

"WHAT?" shouted Dexter.

"The library!" explained Jessica.

"WHAT?!" yelled Dexter.

"Unblock your ears, Dexter!" said Jessica.

"WHAT?!?" bellowed Dexter.

And so the great roar hunt continued as they tiptoed into the library, trying their best not to be heard.

Jessica glanced back. "Whatever you do, Dexter, don't ..." *CLONK!* "... hit your head on the light shade. Or ..."

THUMP! THUMP! THUMP!

"... knock any books off the shelves. Or ..." *SSHHHH!* "... upset the librarian."

Jessica sighed. "Are you sure you're not a clumsy-saurus?!"

SHHH!
A
DICTIONARY
MAPS OF THE WORLD
QUIET PLEASE

D
E
DINO FACTS

They quickly found a comfy spot and started flicking through the dinosaur books.

"Any luck?" asked Jessica.

"Not yet," replied Dexter. "Oh wait, look!"

Jessica peeked round excitedly.

"I think that's a picture of my Uncle Dave in this one!" chuckled Dexter.

Book after book, page after page, they hunted and hunted until Jessica noticed a big blue book tucked away in the corner.

"Hang on, that one's wobbling," said Jessica.

"What. Is. That?" said Dexter.

Jessica took a deep breath and opened it up. A ginormous roar erupted from the pages and whooshed into Dexter's mouth.

"RRRROOOOOAAAAAARRRR!"

"YAAAAYYYY!" cheered Jessica.

"SHHHHHHH!" hissed the librarian.

"ROAR," whispered Dexter happily.

RRRRROOOAAARRR

After a long day of brass band listening, seagull dodging, fire engine riding, puppy playing, library tiptoeing, head clonking and roar finding, Jessica and Dexter headed back home.

"What a roar-some day!" they cheered.

"Yay for roars and dino-snores," thought Jessica as she drifted off to sleep and began to dream of her next BIG adventure....

Maybe I'll...
GO DIVING?

Jessica, look out for more **Mini Adventures** books.
Go to www.orangutanbooks.co.uk

Story by M.K. Scott
Illustrated by Jo Lindley
Designed by Ryan Dunn

orangutan

First published by Orangutan Books in 2019
Hometown World Ltd, 1 Queen Street, Bath BA1 1HE

Visit
www.orangutanbooks.co.uk
Follow us @orangutanbooks

ISBN 978-1-78979-541-7

Printed in Italy
HTW_PO201929

FSC
www.fsc.org
MIX
Paper from
responsible sources
FSC® C023419